Say the Wrong Thing

Stories and Strategies for Racial Justice and Authentic Community

BY DR. AMANDA KEMP

Foreword by Lisa Graustein, M.Ed.

Joy Will Come Press

*For Michael Jamanis whose open heart and open mind
have often pulled me into my own heart.*

*For Great Aunt Bessie,
who is great in wisdom, love and age.*

*For the Tribe of the Heart,
people who stand for Oneness and Justice, who are
consciously co-creating the Great Shift.*

Table Of Contents

Preface

This book is a compilation of some of the most popular posts on my blog "On a Mission to Heal the Planet." In each essay I share my struggles to stand for justice and oneness. I write as an educator, an artist, a parent and a wife. I write as an African American who lives in an interracial family. I write as someone who grew up in the foster care system of New York City in the South Bronx. I have experienced hunger, neglect and incredible privilege at an all girls boarding school. I've had the chance to experience extremes in my lifetime.

When I first published many of these essays as blog posts, I was surprised to find that my stories struck an emotional chord.

People of color told me they felt good to have their experiences articulated. White readers felt invited into an intimate conversation about race that expanded their understanding and hearts. People whom I knew well and others not at all sent me emails and posted comments about their experience. I was thrilled that teachers and college professors were circulating these amongst colleagues and using them in their teaching. Many colleges and schools are aching for a holistic, unifying approach to the conversation and practice of healthy multi-racial community. I hope that this book aids you in that journey.

I have a special place in my heart for teachers who go beyond their subject matter and reach into the hearts of their students. Thank you for loving kids; thank you for believing in the goodness of your students; and thank you for going well beyond normal work hours to help young people develop their voices and passions. At critical moments a teacher encouraged me to write, to perform or to reach higher than I thought I could attain. I grew up in a low- income marginalized community, but certain teachers made me feel special. When I conduct residencies today, I remember these teachers and affirm each young person I meet.

Finally, I hope this collection nurtures each reader's heart. I hope you will see yourself as part of what I call the Tribe of the Heart. This tribe is a multiracial community of folks who know Separation is a lie and who will "die on the hill of Oneness." My mission is to nurture and expand the Tribe to TAKE ACTION to heal the world, our families, and ourselves. As a performing artist, diversity consultant, writer and entrepreneur, I connect my heart to your heart. From the heart, anything can be transformed.

Foreword

In the early 1990's, Alice Walker gathered many of her essays about her social justice work into a book entitled *Anything We Love Can Be Saved*. Throughout the book, Alice Walker shows us, again and again, how stepping fully into the pain and truth of injustice with an open and fiercely directed heart makes space for transformation. Amanda Kemp offers us the same gift and modeling in *Say the Wrong Thing*. Through her reflections, and more importantly, her actions, Amanda offers us a way through the pain of racism to the powerful healing work our world demands of us right now.

Like Alice Walker, Amanda brings to all her work a deep love – for herself, her family, her community, and all people. This is an unflinching love that will speak the hard truths that need to be spoken. It is also a love that invites all of us to step into the space of fuller being – of being more honest, more committed, more vulnerable, and more open to wholeness. In a culture that inoculates us against fully feeling and in which so much communication occurs through brief, inadequate texts, e-mails, and sound bites, Amanda's writing invites us to pause, to feel, to connect, and then move into the greater fullness of who we are and who we can be for each other.

Last August I was preparing to lead a diversity workshop for a group of school staff. The previous time we had met was the day after the South Carolina church shootings, when a third of room sat mute with grief. I wanted some things for people to read before the workshop to spark thinking, to engage people, to acknowledge the pain of the murders over the summer, and to meet the wide range of experiences the staff would be bringing to the space. Amanda's blog was the first place I went. *Staying Healthy When Black Lives Don't Matter* was one of the pieces of writing I selected. It beautifully framed the issues the school needed to address: how do we do the work of teaching and mentoring young people of color in a time and place in which they are told daily their lives don't matter? How do we care for ourselves in this work? How and when do we take the risks to call our colleagues out of ignorance and into deeper understandings of our students' lives and our choices to replicate or change the power structures that keep inequities in place?

Amanda's writings consistently offer the modeling we need: to name what is really happening; to feel, fully, the impact; to connect the current reality to the larger patterns and histories; and to creatively respond in ways that invite truth, healing, and wholeness. The directness, honesty, and clarity of Amanda's writings call us into a deeper and more self-aware place. This is not always an easy place to go, but Amanda's invitation to lead us and stand with us in those places opens up the potential for transformation. *Say the Wrong Thing* is not a pat guide to multicultural appreciation, it is a vibrant, commanding invitation to be the change that we need, right now.

Lisa Graustein,

M.Ed. Racial

Justice Educator

Introduction

Say the Wrong Thing and Strategies of the H.E.A.R.T.

I am sitting at a Starbucks sipping coffee wondering what will happen. Michael and I are going to meet to talk about the violin in INSPIRA, my new performance project; rather we are talking about the possibility of not including the violin. I am angry about Ferguson. I am angry about the complacency of White America in general, and I don't want to worry about offending anyone.

What will I say to this man I love, this white-identified man whose instrument symbolizes Western and Northern European dominance? What can we risk with each other?

I say the hard stuff. I assert my ownership of the project. I say I don't like that it's so "classical." I say that I'm angry, and I'm not toning down my project or partying with people who don't want to honor black life. That he's white hasn't mattered much before, but I've never created a work about now, and now hurts. The country is polarized, and it is so apparent how white people have been trained to devalue Black life. I don't think he's willing to take a controversial stand, and I don't want to accommodate.

Still, I don't want to lose this man; my lover, best friend, and co-parent support. And yet, something is missing, and I don't want to pretend.

He says the hard stuff. He is a violinist, and he's white. He tells me I underestimate him. I do not know him or what he can do with the violin. He's angry at me. He wants to take a stand. He's angry at white supremacy.

He's my fiancé. I'm willing to give him a chance.

In the end, we collaborated to create an edgy, angry, mournful and inspiring piece, INSPIRA. Together with an ensemble of three other people of color, we've been touring INSPIRA for almost two years. Michael totally surprised me with his ability to improvise and change his sound, so that he is sometimes a chaotic siren and sometimes a beautiful melodic line. As Francis Wong, our de facto music director and jazz saxophonist said in a Q&A a few weeks ago, "Michael steps up." I've made no compromises on content or attitude, and in a recent Black History Month performance, where Michael and I performed a duet, I realized that he was beautifully helping me to express the complex heartache, hope and power of former Black Panther Assata Shakur.

Risk saying the wrong thing.

I tell this story because to get to this point, I had to risk saying the wrong thing. I had to risk losing someone I loved by speaking my incomplete truth. None of us has the entire truth, but we've got to voice what is real for us in order for the partnership or the community to advance. I did not know that Michael could change his sound. I did not know he was willing to cross over and feel pain and anger with me. We would never have created such a rich, satisfying collaboration if I had not spoken. Nor would we have done so if he had not spoken his truth and challenged me to let him do his thing.

Recently, I led a training where folks listed the reasons why we don't have authentic conversations about racism. The number one answer was fear of saying the wrong thing. White identified people feared looking stupid or offending. People of color feared losing professional opportunities and alienating other people of color. As an African American woman said, "I'm trying to make sure you don't feel uncomfortable because then I get uncomfortable and think ... how far can I go before I lose my job?"

However, it's not just in our work lives that we fear saying the wrong thing. It's also on the playground, in our faith communities, and in the committees for peace and social change. For example, in another discussion, a white parent shared with me that they could not stop focusing on the fact that another parent at the event in their all white neighborhood was Black. They wanted to bring it up to in be in solidarity with this Black family but said nothing because they feared saying the wrong thing.

Why say the wrong thing?

The fall-out can be tough and uncomfortable, so, why say the wrong thing?

One, the status quo sucks. Have you noticed that we live in a quagmire of fear and judgment buttressed by an unfair justice system, systemic housing, job and education disparity? Have you noticed that a higher percentage of Americans are committing suicide now than have in decades? Our rates of depression, anxiety, and all kinds of disorders show that we live amidst a lot of fear and misery.

According to somatic expert Rusia Mohiuddin, humans require love, connection, and safety. When we let the fear of saying the wrong thing rule us, we may get a semblance of safety but we do not experience deep love or connection. What's especially deadly is that regular withholding from others actually compromises our connection to and love of ourselves. We become habitually inauthentic and unmoored from our center. We wage war on ourselves which gets projected out to other people and group.

Two, your vision of a just, compassionate world is only possible if you take a risk. You could forge a powerful team, long term solution, or success beyond your wildest dreams if you did not let saying the wrong thing stop you. If we stop focusing on looking bad or causing harm, and instead focus on cultivating the capacity to listen and speak from the heart; we will move a lot closer to the world we seek.

I remember when Beth, a white woman at my Quaker meeting whispered to me something like "This is a really white Christmas program, isn't it?" She made it known that she wanted to talk with me about race. I answered and from there, years later, we have an ongoing healing racism working group that raises consciousness about racism within our meeting and is organizing to end mass incarceration. Sometimes it has been messy, but we have hung in there through the mess. The result is far better than if we had played it fake.

Strategies of the H.E.A.R.T.

I subtitled this collection "Stories and Strategies for Racial Justice and Authentic Connection" because I share stories from my life and embedded in the stories are the strategies that I use. I call these strategies of the H.E.A.R.T. for the five step program I've developed to promote justice and oneness. To be clear, I practice these strategies imperfectly, but I have found peace, confidence, and solid ground by using them. Below, I briefly summarize these strategies:

Hold space for transformation: Practice unconditional acceptance of what is and who is

Express yourself: Share from the heart.

Act with intention: Take action even if it is imperfect.

Reflect on yourself: Cultivate self-awareness

Trust the process: Let yourself and others be uncomfortable. Be gentle with yourself as you grow.

I've grouped the essays into these five strategies, but this book is not theoretical or abstract. You will see me groping my way. You will see that I get triggered and upset. I cause suffering. I back down. I get back up. I write about being a dark brown, African American woman living in a predominantly white nation, whose structures regularly and historically degrade Black people. I write about how I have internalized those pernicious messages.

I make art in a predominantly Black, multi-racial ensemble and regularly perform with my husband. I facilitate "diversity and justice" workshops and consult with organizations who want to be "diverse." I write about loving a white-identified man and parenting African American children. I include a personal narrative by my son Gabriel Anthony-Kemp whose experience as a Black young man has spurred my commitment to make schools and our world more just. My life is messy and my growth uneven, but these strategies work.

Finally, thank you for reading this book. Thank you for helping to create a new tribe of people who are willing to notice and share their imperfection as they journey toward justice and oneness. In her Ted Talk, Verna Myers says "We don't need good people; we need real people." I could not agree more. I hope this book inspires you to be real. It is time to affirm a new tribe, a tribe of the heart.

Hold Space for Transformation

Practice unconditional acceptance of what is and who is.

Out beyond ideas of wrongdoing and rightdoing,

there is a field. I'll meet you there.

When the soul lies down in that grass,

the world is too full to talk about.

Ideas, language, even the phrase "each other"
doesn't make any sense.

mevlana jelaluddin rumi
13th century poet and mystic

In other words, we are holding a space where
each person can see and acknowledge the injustice in and upon
which we currently live while also remembering
our divine birthright and deep interconnection.

Niyonu Spann
Founder Beyond Diversity 101

We Are Here for All of Us,
NO EXCEPTIONS!

I love the Alicia Keys song "We Are Here." I am partial to visionaries, and in this song she sings the impossible: "We are here for all of us...that's why we are here."

My soul loves the challenge in this song. We are here for each other whether we are Syrians detained in Hungary or a teenager locked in solitary confinement on Rikers Island. We are here for all of us. None of us gets left out. As I sing along, I know the truth of her statement, but the tears well up because the gap between that truth and this reality seems infinite.

Are *we really* here *for all of us? How about the folks doing Rebel Runs in Lancaster County to support the Confederate flag? How about the people who kill children in Gaza or Nigeria?*

Am I here for all of us? Am I here for the police who arrested and knocked African American tennis player James Blake to the ground even though he repeatedly told them who he was? Am I here for the clerk in Alabama who does not want to marry same sex couples?

I know these folks aren't here for me, but in the face of this reality, Alicia still sings:

We are here...
We are here *for all*
of us We are here
for all of us That's
why we're here.

How do I pray for the dominating and overpowering? Based on my early childhood experience of domestic violence, I automatically feel for the underdog. If it's David and Goliath, I'll side with David every time.

Yet Alicia's song invites us to another order of logic, another paradigm, the paradigm of Oneness.

When I'm feeling grateful and safe, this paradigm of Oneness seems obvious and superior to Separation. However, when I'm angry and feeling abandoned, Alicia's invitation doesn't even occur to me. I'm automatically in Separation.

Because I'm human, I've got to cultivate the capacity to see, hear and ACT from the space of "We are here for all of us." It does not come naturally. My brain's default is threat and defense; judgment and separation. To cultivate Alicia's song requires practice and forgiveness.

Two Ways We Can Cultivate Oneness

Hold Space for Transformation

I once heard Transformation Leader Niyonu Spann describe holding space as being in a consciousness of active unconditional acceptance, a space of prayer...

When I hold space, I adopt a mindset akin to the Sufi poet Rumi beyond wrongdoing and rightdoing. I listen with loving kindness to all parties and all parts of me. Holding space is a wide embrace of the possibility of transformation of the situation and the players inside it.

Practice Mindfulness

Mindfulness is just practicing bringing all of you into the present moment. "We are here" refers to accepting all of you: your mind, body and heart/spirit. When you practice being present with yourself, you are practicing Oneness and expanding your capacity for holding.

We are in this together. All of us!

Heaven or Hell?

I haven't believed in a location called hell since I encountered my first atheist at age fourteen. She was an effervescent French girl who wore loads of make up and used Evian to cool herself down when she got too excited. I grew to love Elsa, but was anxious for her soul when she announced there was no God. That she did not get struck down immediately shocked me almost as much as her pronouncement.

Since then, I've lived with Hell as a state of Separation, or as Satre said: "Hell is other people." For example:

People who cut you off in traffic.

Police you can't trust.

Ex-spouses.

Your children (sometimes).

People who don't hold the door for you.

Your boss.

Your direct

report. Your

kid's teacher.

The person in front of you at the check-out.

"Other people" are everywhere. I love "Hell is other people" because it points to inevitable suffering when we see ourselves as separate from "other people." At any given moment we can choose hell, separating ourselves from "others" who harm us or those we love. We can make "other people" the problem, the threat, and the only thing separating us from contentment.

It makes sense. People do crappy things to each other. Systems encourage individuals to separate and harm each other. It makes sense to fight back. It makes sense to accept the us vs. them equation especially when the other side clearly sees me as a "them" to exterminate.

Yet, I've got this thread, an unbreakable thin line connected to my heart that says: We can't win this game. If the solution is only more Separation, then we keep losing. As Brother Martin famously said "an eye for an eye leaves us all blind." What then can we do?

This is where I turn to Spirit, an inner grace that allows me to connect and be compassionate even as I fight for a just world. When I'm ready for a little taste of heaven, I meditate, pray for the willingness to forgive, and/or practice self-compassion, all of which take me closer to God.

Lean In

What do you do when somebody says something classic like: "This country is so focused on racism that we're forgetting about everybody else"?

As a justice and diversity consultant, I encounter some version of this all the time. Sometimes it will also pop up in a one on one conversation in my personal life. Today I want to highlight a strategy that artist Ricardo Levins Morales suggested in the Deeper Change Forum a few weeks ago. Ricardo urged us to seek the common ground of values even when we disagree with each others' narratives.

Recently, I heard a European American who felt worn out by the constant scramble to earn a living and get impatient with charges of racism. It's almost like he/she said "Hey, my life is sucking right now too, but I don't get to play the race card. I just have to keep working harder, and nobody cares."

Typically, I walk away from someone who takes that position because I feel disregarded, dismissed and just plain "dissed."

Even now, I notice that my belly feels tight and my breathing got shallow just writing and imagining scenarios where this has played out. Walking away is a legit option, especially when you are on Facebook.

When I feel vulnerable or angry, I'm not in the head space to look for the shared values. So, I typically remove myself.

However, when this happened recently, I leaned in, breathed a little deeper and asked questions. Here is the flavor of the questions that I posed. I did not do this perfectly so I comment on each question as to its effectiveness.

Can both be true? Can there be racism and your life be really frustrating because you're on a grind where things just aren't getting better?

This is a great question if the person isn't in too much pain. I asked it out of my frustration. May or may not be a great first question.

What's frustrating you about your job?

This is a great question because it's better to get right to the cause of the person's pain. The real issue is not whether or not African Americans have it better than European Americans.

The person's real issue is: I'm scared, frustrated, and tired, and I feel alone in carrying all this. Somebody please care about me. This is where I can find the shared value: You and I are both a child of God and worthy of a great life, as are our children. I'm on your side too. We're on the same side.

Can I share what it's like for me?

This is the part I downplayed a bit too much. However, it's progress for me that I risked to share any of what I was feeling and noticing. Sometimes I go into social worker mode to avoid being vulnerable. In this case I validated that racism hurts and isolates.

What's your heart saying right now? What's my heart saying right now?

Let's take care of each others' hearts. The quickest way to shift the mind (which is built for separation and defense) is to go straight to the heart. Asking what the heart says could help to navigate around the ego.

Our conversation could have easily ended with a stalemate and separation. Instead we traveled toward each other because the questions were not aiming to disprove the person's narrative about racism. Rather, I went to fundamental shared experience of frustration and inadequacy. The conversation went the way of shared values: I care about you and want to know what's hard for you right now. Your feelings are important to me. I share my feelings with you.

Finally, as I said before, when we engage is a choice. If your heart needs comfort, then you may not have the space to meet someone where they are. Don't sacrifice yourself. Instead nurture yourself. Meditate. Take a bath. Get a hug from a trusted someone—like your dog. You will get another chance to engage someone who makes that kind of comment—sooner or later.

Express
YOURSELF

Share from the heart.

*In the cause of silence, each of us draws
the face of her own fear — fear of contempt, of censure,
of some judgment, or recognition, of challenge, of annihilation.
But most of all, I think, we fear
the visibility without which we cannot truly live.*

Audre Lorde

Staying Healthy
WHEN BLACK LIVES DON'T MATTER.

When I see yet another email about the killing of a Black human being; when I see yet another video on Facebook about a Black woman being threatened; when I am asked to sign yet another online petition asking the Justice Dept. to protect Black children--I feel like throwing up, raging, and crying.

You, too, might be feeling this way. In fact you might experience post-traumatic stress disorder--if you don't take steps to care for yourself. According to *The Washington Post*, we can experience vicarious trauma as we encounter degradation of Black life on our social media feeds. A Black psychologist recommends unplugging for a while if you start to get overwhelmed.

I urge you to go a step further.

Please write out how you feel. Just set a timer and write without stopping, editing, arguing, or censoring.

I did this and found out that the societal violence against Black women and girls was triggering my old wounds. The video of the police and Sandra Bland and the photos of the young teen who was thrown to the ground in a two-piece bathing suit while the policeman put his knee in her back and pulled her hair hurt me. These videos took me back emotionally to times when my voice did not matter, when my "No" was ignored, when I could not breathe. I let this free association flow onto the page.

Writing *it out gives us a chance to bear witness to our experience and to comfort ourselves. After I wrote, I* recorded *myself reading it.* Later, *I* shared *what I had written with my husband Michael.*

Later still, I began to share *it with two friends after meditating. I prayed for guidance. And it got* lighter. *I didn't have to* share *the whole piece.*

Now I'm going to work on it as a spoken word performance piece called #Say Her Name.

The first step is to care for yourself and notice what is happening in you. You may choose to stay away from social media or the news for a while. Write out your feelings--not about your feelings. Share with someone(s) you trust.

In these traumatic times we must know what's going on AND we must care for ourselves. Let's not mirror this larger society's degradation of Black life. Let's tend to ourselves.

From My Son; to My Son

On Dec. 20, 2015 I received an email from my son. As I read it, I wept and marveled at his clarity. Over the weeks, I wrote several responses. Below, I start with excerpts from his narrative, and then I share my attempt to have "The Talk" in writing.

From My Son

Mom, take a look at this. I wrote it at 3 am today. I wrote it not knowing where it would take me. By the time I got to the end, I had diagnosed myself and identified my problem. —Gabe

> *There is a piece of me that doesn't allow certain things to slide. That piece is embedded in my soul and I haven't figured out how to control it.*

> *At least once a month I see a video of a Black man beaten and or killed by police. My parents and loved ones tell me to be careful. They tell me to do things I shouldn't have to do, but if I want to*

26

survive I have to listen. I have to make sure I'm not a threat because if I make someone scared or uncomfortable they can shoot me. They can shoot my ass and get away with it.

I've been internalizing these messages for the last four years, and it's changing my body. It's changing my brain and my emotions. It's making me go into survival mode where I, a human being, become an animal because that's what I'm constantly told I am and how I see people like me being treated. It is beginning to be too much to cope with at times.

People say things, or I watch a video of a handcuffed man's head being kicked like a football by a white dude with a badge. These things flip a switch. My body feels like it's going to detonate when it's reminded that where I live I'm not safe. I don't have the same human experience as white people. I have to be on the lookout constantly, like prey in the wild. When I'm triggered, I don't have control of my body. When an animal is running from a predator, it's not thinking about anything else except survival. I am sixteen years old, and I know that feeling.

I had the feeling a couple weeks ago. Someone said something about another black person being taken to a secret police interrogation site and tortured to death in Chicago. I had a mug in my hand, and my hand starting shaking so badly that I dropped the mug. My heart began to beat furiously and my face got tight. I ground my teeth and couldn't be still. I went into a mode where I felt like an animal that had had enough and was going to try and destroy my predator. In this situation it felt like my predators were white students at this school saying racism is not a thing anymore. I can't just go and hurt little innocent white children that don't know that they just hurt my feelings. I ran and starting punching and kicking things. I hurt myself. I punched until I couldn't feel my right hand and my arm was covered in blood. It was raining, and I was muddy and bloody. I sat down in the mud, and just cried. I didn't cry because of any physical pain... I cried because I knew what was happening. I cried because I knew it was just going to get worse. I don't know how much longer my human body and brain can take feeling like an animal.

Lately, just pounding ideas has become harder and harder. I find myself getting upset and wanting to dismantle the ideas but also dismantle things. Tangible things. I want to hit things and break them. I want to see people hurt because they don't give a fuck what's going on around them. They don't give a fuck that I am in pain every single day because my humanity isn't valued. I want them to feel a fraction of the pain I feel daily. I want them to look in my eyes and see the hurt. I want them to know that in this society my body and my mind are less than theirs, and because of that I'm disposable. I'm just another Nigga that can be shot and killed without any consequences.

I am being reconfigured as a human being. Humans adapt to survive. I feel like I'm adapting to become an animal, an animal in constant danger. I don't know what to do about it.

To My Son #1

Dear Gabriel,

America hates Black men. Just below the surface, underground, a fierce well of fear and hatred boils and roils against Black men and boys. It also erupts against Black girls and women, but there is a gendered dimension to the fear of Black men.

I see the vitriol against Barack Obama and professional athletes as eruptions of subconscious white fear and anxiety. I do not want it to be so, but it is. No matter how professional, positive, and accomplished we are, Black people, as a group, are not good enough, not innocent enough, not American enough.

You rage against the way this game is stacked, and rightly so. Jay Smooth says "Race is a dance partner who is designed to trip you up." It's not biological but it is real—as real as getting arrested for a traffic stop and then turning up dead in police custody two days later.

To My Son #2

Dear Gabriel,

I want you to know your writing pierced my heart, and you matter to me and to the world.

Your letter tells me that we, the adults in your life, must do more. As an adult, I can stop co-signing white complacency in the midst of an unbearable status quo. I can ask white people who love me to see this reality, this unbearable state of affairs, and take a stand. I can bring up the elephant of racism when it's in the room. I can be uncomfortable more often.

I realize that I avoid feeling the pain of the women who've lost their beautiful Black children. My consciousness touches on the incredible anger and grief of these women, and I flinch. I quickly move away. But today I'm promising: I will write. I will create. I will acknowledge them.

To My Son #3

Dear Gabriel,

I'm writing again.

Franz Fanon said: "Every generation must ... discover its mission, fulfill it, or betray it."

As your mother, I want you to live. "Be safe" I command you almost automatically when you leave the house. But what's the cost of living "safe"? The cost is too high if you feel like you've got to keep your head down, rather than up; if you feel you are always under threat and can't breathe fully. It's definitely too high if you experience yourself as prey, hunted and not quite human.

You are not prey.

To God, you are an infinite being of light, capable of mighty works in service to all living beings.

To me, you are my beautiful Black boy who is coming into manhood.

To our ancestors, my mother and her mother, you are the extension of a lineage of powerful people. My grandmother, your great grandmother, was a leader in the NAACP and on the frontline of the civil rights movement in Mississippi. Your great, great Aunt Bessie challenged segregation in Georgia by herself when she

was only in her early 20s. You are the inheritor of our line's ase (Yoruba for "the power to make things happen") and you now must choose how to use it.

Listen to your deepest self. Sink down to your deepest self. Whatever action you take from that space will be true and powerful and right.

Love,

Mama Bear (a.k.a. Amanda)

Act with Intention

Take action even if it is imperfect.

Desiring to justify himself and to show that Jesus' reply was far from conclusive, the lawyer asks, "And who is my neighbour?" The lawyer was now taking up the cudgels of debate that might have turned the conversation into an abstract theological discussion. But Jesus, determined not to be caught in the "paralysis of analysis," pulls the question from mid air and places it on a dangerous curve between Jerusalem and Jericho.

Martin Luther King, Jr.

"It's the action, not the fruit of the action, that's important. You have to do the right thing. It may not be in your power, may not be in your time, that there'll be any fruit. But that doesn't mean you stop doing the right thing. You may never know what results come from your action. But if you do nothing, there will be no result."

Mahatma Gandhi

My Mistake

Do you remember the demonstrations at malls, court houses and hospitals where people staged die-ins? I remember dropping to the ground when the signal came. I remember the slow passage of time as the Park City Mall quieted, and all I heard was my heart.

When I arose, I looked up to see my fifteen year old son and his best friend. I was stunned. I had not known if there would be arrests or conflicts with counter-protestors so I had not told him about it.

My mistake.

I wanted to protect him. I had told myself I couldn't guarantee his safety. There had been threats from people who hated Black Lives Matter movements. We didn't know for sure how the police would deal with us. Would they let us disperse? "Better not bring my son or any of my children," I told myself.

But what was I teaching my son? "You are a target. Keep your head down. Let mommy take the chances. Don't you stand up."

My mistake.

Months later when people traveled to Baltimore to hold the City accountable for killing Freddie Gray. My son called me.

"Take me to Baltimore."

"Why Baltimore?" I asked. "What do you want to do there?"

"People are protesting. It's happening there, Mommy!"

This time I did not say no, but I did not say yes.

"Wait!" I said. "Let me call around."

I consulted my friend who had supported organizers and movements in Ferguson. Safety was my first concern. "Tell me that it's too unpredictable to go," I begged silently. My friend gave me no such advice. Instead he offered very practical advice about where to stand and what to look for in an unpredictable situation confronting public officials, including the police.

I waited a few days to call my son back. By then, other high school matters were on his mind. Soon after, the prosecutor announced her plan to indict the officers.

I felt relieved. I had kept him safe.

Yet, a small part of me knew that we had missed an opportunity.

Recently, my son sent me a short narrative that exposed his anguish, rage, and sense of impotence at the fact that Black Lives Don't Matter much too often. I wept as I read his outpouring. (See previous chapter.)

"So, what are we to tell our beautiful Black and Brown boys? As a mother, my instincts scream "Keep the child safe!"

But if he does not participate in demonstrations, group actions and even risk arrest, how will he know that he is powerful? How will he know that he is not just an extension of what the dominant society says?

Tonight, I'm going to screen the first play that I've written where my son said: "It made me feel like I had to go out and freaking do something!"

The play, "To Cross an Ocean Four Centuries Long" features an enslaved woman, Hannah, who lost her son. I was entrusted with her story after wrestling with the autobiography of Quaker abolitionist, John Woolman. She came to me while I slept. I

resisted because there were no documents to back up her story. But

finally, I got up around 4 am and wrote her story. Her grief and her adaptation to that loss wrenched my heart. She could not keep her boy safe.

Tonight we will screen the filmed version of the play. I will once again cry with Hannah. I will think about the mothers of Tamir Rice, Trayvon Martin, and Mike Brown.

I will think about my son.

However, this time I will think about how I will support him. This time I will encourage him to resist, to act.

When You Lose YOUR POWER

Have you ever been somewhere and just had to write down what someone said so that you could look at it again later?

Last week I kept writing as I listened to self-described "political artist" and long-time organizer Ricardo Levins Morales speak at the Deeper Change Forum in New Haven, CT. Ricardo spoke about trauma.

Trauma & Medicine

Ricardo spoke of trauma, at its essence, as a loss of power; someone or something taking away your ability to protect or act. Having experienced this loss, we instinctively self-medicate. We do something to remove ourselves from the shame, pain, etc. The medicine we take may strengthen or poison us.

Almost simultaneously, I thought of the group and individual levels in which this plays out. For African Americans, the trauma of slavery, jim crow, segregation, and second-class citizenship is enforced by state violence, lynch mobs, and individuals such as George Zimmerman. The threat is always there. As a group we tend to experience police killing of black men and women, boys and girls as a stripping of our power. We experience today's Confederate flag as a reminder of our severe loss of power as humans under slavery. We are frequently re-traumatized on social media. Not surprisingly, we collectively and individually take medicine to numb the pain and/or to restore our power.

Take Your Medicine!

I see the Black Lives Matter movement as an example of medicine that restores power. Instead of internalizing the shame, people left their individual homes and took to communal spaces such as the streets, courthouses, hospitals, schools, shopping malls, etc. to say no more shame on us, it's shame on you. Moreover, we exercised power as a group to demand the Attorney General, the President, the Prosecutors, the mayors, etc. take action to protect and nurture Black life. These demonstrations of power were often angry and fierce and led by younger generations.

I also see art created by groups such as Tribe One and my own Inspira: The Power of the Spiritual as medicine. I went to a Tribe One concert last November soon after a New York grand jury failed to indict the officers who killed Eric Garner.

Tribe One sang songs of hope and grief and then created a song with the audience about what they were feeling and knowing. Using phrases like "No justice, no peace," "I can't breathe" and "truth and reconciliation;" Tribe One created art that bound our wounds and reinforced our oneness.

Similarly, as part of Inspira, Matthew Armstead and I shared journal entries written during the Ferguson uprising and used chants from protests to build a soundscape along with our musical improvisation.

These performances provided space for us to feel our anger, grief, despair, and remember our power to do good. They resonated with audiences deeply because people already know they can affect reality but, as Ricardo says, "we've been brutalized into forgetting."

Conscious Self-Medication

Ricardo's words also made me think of my individual trauma: childhood neglect and sexual abuse. As a child I coped with the loss of power by escaping into novels. My medicine was to read anything we had in the house for hours. I also developed a highly self-critical voice as I strove to be "good." Feeling unsafe, I couldn't sleep at night. I also denied sadness and anger and put on a "happy face." These strategies helped in the short term, but led to a mental health crisis when I was fifteen. Today, when I get triggered, I automatically go back to these standbys.

Thankfully, I've also developed some new ways to remember my power to protect and befriend myself. For example, I drink a lot of hot water. In fact, I take a hot bath two or three times a week. I also write out my feelings. I share with a trusted friend. And, thanks to the 30

Day Meditation Challenge, I now meditate as a way to reboot. However, I'm not too proud to say that I take myself to a professional and cry it all out when the Big Feelings get triggered and I feel destabilized. Like the artist and the change-maker, a counselor can render the invisible visible and accompany you back to your core.

Here's a challenge to you: Notice when you feel as if your power has been stripped away from you. What triggered you? Consciously choose your medicine. Here's a little loving kindness meditation that I repeat silently for five minutes.

May I be well.

May I be happy.

May I be free from suffering.

Don't be stubborn; take your medicine!

SAY HER NAME,
Inspira and Art as Ceremony

I'm writing just after spending a week as Friend-in-Residence at Haverford College. It was a huge week of meeting professors, speaking with students at Quaker House, leading workshops, sharing meals and teaching classes. You might expect this as a Friend-in-Residence. What was unexpected was the end of the week performance-ceremony, #SayHerName. (This hashtag was created to highlight the killing of Black women while in police custody.)

Quaker Affairs asked me to share so that folks might get a taste of me as a performer. As I was preparing, I realized I really wanted to experiment with ceremony. Could we effectively use ritual and performance to make ourselves and the community more whole?

YES! Together we created #SayHerName, part-performance, part-ritual to make visible the killing of Black women by police and while in police custody.

We began by acknowledging that which we hold divine and our ancestors. People shared names of about a dozen ancestors, and we could have gone on, but I drew it to a close so that we could continue.

Next, I used elements from Ricardo Levins Morales, and we acknowledged the oppressive power relationships and ideologies in the room. "Patriarchy, we recognize you but we do NOT submit to you. White supremacy, we recognize you but we do NOT submit to you."

We also called in what we wanted to assist us in the space. "Courage, we honor you, and we welcome you. Hope, we honor you, and we welcome you." It was such a relief to acknowledge crappy ideologies without submitting to them. Similarly, it felt good to call in the values that strengthened us.

I then shared film clips of monologues written about real women who had endured slavery. We listened to their stories.

Things got really tense after I shared an audio recording of a spoken word piece that I wrote while gripped in pain over the killing of Sandra Bland. We also watched a slideshow of other women recently killed by the police or while in custody. Michael Jamanis and Francis Wong from the "INSPIRA: The Power of the Spiritual" ensemble improvised beautiful music that morphed into a fiery jazz explosion as Matthew Armstead sang "No justice, no peace," and Gerri McCritty brought in the dun-dun drums.

Afterward people stayed to share their hearts, their commitment to take action and their appreciation. A prospective freshman, a young Black woman, stayed a long time to tell me that she'd never experienced anything like that and was inspired to follow her calling.

I share this because this is why I continue working as an artist. Art creates space where we can experience our Oneness despite the systemic oppression that separates and dehumanizes us. I am being used to get to the heart of the matter.

Some of us do policy research and advocacy. Some of us organize marches, die-in's, and other direct actions. Some of us pray and meditate and send energy to all of the folks on the frontlines. This is all important and good.

My work feeds the tribe of people who remember we are One, the Tribe of the Heart.

Reflect on
YOURSELF
Cultivate self-awareness.

*As our mindfulness practice deepens we become more aware
of our thoughts. This offers us the opportunity to assess them
and notice that much of the time our thoughts are
not really serving us. Many thoughts are driven by fear
and lock us into insecurity. During our residential meditation
retreats, one of the biggest breakthroughs people share with us is:
"I realized I don't have to believe my thoughts."*

Tara Brach

*Courage of heart will allow us to see and make these difficult
acknowledgements, record the truth of them, but then also to take
the necessary action, both within and without, to right them.*

Niyonu Spann

WALKING While BLACK

It could have been any usual morning, except it was not. This morning, after my usual high protein breakfast of black beans, salmon, salad, and a bite of eggs, I set out on my fifteen-minute brisk walk.

I don't like to be cold–except when I'm heat flashing-so I added a mid-thigh, black suede coat to my ensemble.

I start walking. I see a white family of three or four kids and two adults playing while waiting for the school bus.

Immediately, I feel weird. I feel like a threat. I am Black, dark brown. I have dread locks. I am wearing a black coat that could conceal something bad.

This is not my neighborhood, not my state and not my home. I am an outsider. I am in a middle class neighborhood in Hamden, Connecticut.

No one in the family speaks, and I keep my eyes forward so as not to offend or be offended. I feel fear.

It is 8:25am. I worry that someone will call the police about a suspicious Black woman walking.

As I walk, I wish I had chosen my lime green sweater. It's cute and it seems to increase my innocence.

Black is dangerous. It hides things. I'm dangerous. I could be hiding something.

These are the automatic thoughts that I notice myself thinking only after I pass another collection of white adults and children waiting for the school bus. As I pass this group, a woman smiles and says "Good morning." I respond "Good morning" and smile back. A little. I keep walking.

Going down a steep hill, I realize I've internalized all of these messages about Black people, about myself as a threat. I pick up speed. There's nothing wrong with me, I insist, still worried about my black, mid-thigh, suede coat that a white friend had given to me. You're going to be okay, I tell myself. I search for a hair band to tie up my dreads. No luck.

As I turn around to ascend the hill, I open the coat. There, nobody will think I'm hiding a weapon. I'm wearing a pink fitted sweater and an olive cardigan underneath my jacket. I am innocently female. (I know #SayHerName, but I'm just doing what I can.)

As I huff and puff my way to the top of the hill, I feel a little relieved that all the families are gone. I don't feel like a threat.

Still, I practice what I will say to the police: I'm visiting my friend ……… and her address is ……… I'm proud that I remember her address.

I worry about my so n, about black boys and men who walk outside their neighborhoods. Threatening. Suspicious. Trayvon Martin sits in the back of my consciousness. I worry that they don't have female innocence to draw on, a cute lime green sweater or a fitted pink top to cue the outside world that they are not a threat. (Of course, that did not save Sandra Bland.)

A car speeds toward me. I am facing traffic. There's no sidewalk here. People who walk are unexpected. Will the dark coat hide me from a careless, momentarily distracted driver? I jump to the side.

I arrive home.

I go to the guest

bedroom. I meditate.

I write.

This is what it's like to "Walk while Black."

If You're Black, JUMP BACK?

If you're white, you're all

right. If you're brown,

hang around. If you're

black, jump back.

children's rhyme

If you are unprepared to encounter interpretations that you might find objectionable, please do not proceed further.

Harvard University Implicit Association Test

I was a tornado of a little girl. I had lots of energy and imagination. I made up songs and dramas and acted them out −by myself if no one was around or wanted to play with me.

I loved the social life and the intellectual challenge of elementary school. I can't remember not knowing how to read. I loved nap time in kindergarten. I loved cookies for jobs completed in first grade. I loved

49

my second grade teacher's turban and long arm of bracelets. She was light brown and bought me a notebook.

I did not like being Black. I did not like my dark brown skin color. I did not like the jokes, the criticisms, and the presumption that I was not pretty because I was "dark-skinned."

"Don't turn off the lights; we'll never find Amanda!" would always get a laugh.

I wasn't good at put-downs so I would smile and pretend I did not care. I felt guilty as charged. I was Black. I didn't know of any insults for being brown, tan, yellow, coffee colored, etc.

I grew up in the 1970s in a predominantly Black neighborhood with a sizable Puerto Rican and Latino population. It was an insult to call someone "black." I remember someone saying: "I'm not Black; I'm brown."

Yes, this was the time of James Brown's "Say it Loud, I'm Black and I'm Proud," but it was also the time of only lighter-skinned women being featured as *Jet* magazine's "Beauty of the Week."

All of the new Black television shows and movies of the 1970s featured women who were lighter skinned –unless they were playing asexual, mammy characters. Think "Julia" or even "Raisin in the Sun."

To comfort me, my foster mother would say "Don't you worry, baby; you're getting lighter every day." I was the only dark brown girl in the family. I hoped she was right because the only other dark brown person in the house was my foster brother, a teen who was always in trouble.

Eventually, I started fighting back. In junior high, a group of boys would pick a girl they thought was ugly and scream at her in the hallway while we changed classes. I'd watched them do it to several girls–all dark brown. I was in the smart class. I had glasses. I had crooked teeth. And, most importantly I was Black. I waited for my turn.

When they finally screamed at me, I just kept walking as if I didn't see them. I don't know if my friends were with me, but I felt alone.

One of the boys stepped in front of me and said something, and I opened my mouth:

"You're no dreamboat yourself" came out.

I kept walking.

All of his friends laughed. They were shocked an "ugly girl" had hit back. They were shocked at my word choice. I know because they said so.

Later, when I was in my final year of junior high, a boy shouted as I passed by "you look like an African queen."

Now in my neighborhood, even if we had mostly gotten to the point of not denying we were Black, we were emphatically NOT African.

Notwithstanding the Black nationalists, the Nation of Islam, and other folks countering the narrative of Africa as a dark continent, most people in my world did not respect, value or claim any connection to Africa.

Therefore, when he put 'African" in front of queen; I heard it as mockery.

My response: "That's the best kind."

I tell you these stories because I've battled to see my skin color as sensual, rich, and one of my best features. I have fought despair and loneliness when I was passed over because I was too dark.

When I read about dark brown women characters choosing navy and brown clothes so as not to draw attention to our skin, I went out and bought yellows, reds, pinks, and white.

After I graduated from college, I was approached by my friend Luis, a Mexican American. I tried to explain my hesitance to date him. I liked him. A lot. He was really cute and artistic. "But," I said, very gently "I'm really Black." I'll never forget his reaction. He literally fell down on the hiking trail in laughter. I tried again: "I am not a 'by the way' Black person." (I love this story and promise to write about what happened after that another time.)

I am now almost fifty. Studies show that colorism and white supremacy persist, but I resist. I have degrees and certifications in African & Afro-American Studies and African Studies. I've taught

Africana Studies, classes on whiteness, and post-colonialism. I've lived on the Continent, organized Black students, represented Black community interests, and organized in support of African liberation movements. I've built an identity around actively fighting for Black Art, Black complexity, Black traditions, Black intellectual history.

Therefore, I approached Harvard's implicit bias test with high awareness of color preference in our society. I chose the Skin-Tone Implicit Bias Test without a lot of forethought. Ten minutes later I got my results. I had a moderate "preference for light-skin relative to dark-skin."

Despair.

I had battled and lost. My unconscious, the realm out of my control, had learned "If you're black, jump back."

I did not like my results. Yes, I had grown up in a white supremacist society. Yes, I'd gotten messages my entire life, all around me every day that light is better than dark; white is better than black; etc.

It's understandable, but still, I did not like my results. Immediately questions rose:

My children: one brown, one tan. Do I prefer the tan child?

My stepchildren: two blondes, one brunette. Do I prefer the blondes?

My husband: blue green eyes, grey-white hair, white skin. Do I prefer white men? Light men?

I do not like these questions.

> *If you're white, you're all*
>
> *right. If you're brown, hang*
>
> *around. If you're black, jump*
>
> *back.*

But I sit with them.

I commit again to find and declare the Good, Beautiful, Powerful, Smart, and Lovely in Blackness, in dark-brown people.

Trust the Process

**Let others and yourself be uncomfortable.
Be gentle with yourself as you grow.**

Never place a period where God has placed a comma.

Gracie Allen

B'lieve I'll run on (See What the End's Going to Be).

African American Traditional

PRAY FOR ME

This morning, I was sketching out my day when Michael arrived and said, "Aren't you going to watch the pope?" I hadn't intended to, but I wanted to spend a little time with my very busy husband so I sat to watch the pope speak to Congress. I tuned in and out until the pope went outside to wave at a crowd. Speaking in his native Spanish, he said "Pray for me" and asked those who did not believe or could not pray to send him good wishes.

I've always liked this pope for his economic justice advocacy, but after hearing him ask regular people to pray for him I opened my heart to Pope Francis. I still disagree with him on significant issues, but his humility dissolved my self-righteousness. When he asked me to pray for him, he made himself vulnerable– not perfect, all-seeing or impervious. Like me, he needs prayer. He's in a little boat making big waves, and sometimes we all lose direction.

Watching the pope and discussing this with Michael afterward made me late for an event featuring acclaimed playwright Suzan-Lori Parks.

I almost skipped it, but something told me to just go. As I walked into a warm college gym, Suzan-Lori was demonstrating what she called Radical Inclusion. With her arms stretched open so wide that they were behind her a bit, she demonstrated that radical inclusion requires opening the heart to the point of some discomfort. Radical inclusion means stretching to see some of ourselves in those we don't like or with whom we profoundly disagree. Then a student asked what do you do when you are low or stop believing in your dream. Without skipping a beat, Sister-Girl said "Pray." She suggested something short such as "God, gosh (or whoever), help!" That exchange also took me into my heart. It's as if Suzan-Lori was saying take your sad, hurt, fearful self into your heart. You will find help.

I approached Suzan-Lori after her talk and told her that minutes earlier the pope had asked for prayer, and she hugged me.

Whether you believe in a Higher Power, God, Goddess or divinity; whether you like or dislike this pope; you can allow someone into your strong beautiful heart and "pray" for them or send them "good wishes." When we allow others into our hearts, we are called into our hearts, and from the heart we can transform anything.

I'm praying for you, Francis!

HOW TO GET BACK UP
After You Fall

Do you remember that moment in "The Matrix" when Trinity falls and is too terrified to move? She tells herself "Get up, Trinity, get up!" She jumps up, and she moves, risking her life to save her life.

Well, there I was lying in bed last night after a failed conversation with a very important person. My thinking was getting me more and more anxious and was weighing me down. Thoughts like: "I shouldn't have… I'm screwing up… I'm gonna lose them…" You get the flavor!

And then I started doing what Tara Brach calls the "Two wings of awareness." She says notice what you are experiencing—feelings and physical sensations. As you distinguish each one, gently and lovingly accept each one. Noticing is the masculine wing. Accepting with love (not necessarily approving but accepting what's there in a soft way) is the feminine wing. Do them together and you get back into the present.

So I noticed I was feeling alone. Yes to feeling alone. I noticed I was feeling mad. Yes to feeling mad. I noticed I was feeling scared. Yes, I accept feeling scared. Then I noticed that I felt safe. Yes to safe.

Shortly after, I fell asleep which typically would NOT have happened without distracting myself.

This morning I talked with the important person and admitted that I was trapped by my thoughts. I shared some of the flavor. I said I was sorry for causing suffering. I got defensive. I noticed I was defending and said that out loud too. I noticed my chest felt heavy, and I GOT UP. Then it hit me. I'm defending from my own self- condemnation.

I paused to practice noticing again:

I feel sad. Okay sad.

I feel with myself. Okay with myself.

I feel anxious. Okay anxious.

When you fall, get up. Notice your feelings. Befriend yourself. Listen for your next actions.

Is It Time To
TRASH YOUR MANTRA?

Do you have a subconscious mantra that drives you to despair or panic? Check out how I uncovered mine and adopted a new one instead.

I am onstage, performing the final words of "Say Her Name," a poem that mourns the killing of Sandra Bland. I have no one to sing me through the despair. My friend Vanessa could not come. I have not asked anyone else. In the silence that followed the poem, the spiritual "Hush" comes to me. I sing it alone while the audience holds its breath and watches my pain. I feel alone and vulnerable.

Later, while talking with my friend Matthew, I realized the missing element was community. I had not invited the audience to sing; I had not invited the formation of community. I had been afraid no one would join me.

Two days later, I sing, "Hush" at the end of this poem again. This time twelve women from Haverford College's Outskirts file onto stage, harmonizing behind me. A young Black woman with a smoky alto voice stands beside me and takes the lead. We sing together. She steadies the pace and the pitch. The women behind us blend softly and then loudly, rolling the sound out into the audience. I ask people to stand and sing. They do. Together we ask "Oh, my Lord, oh my Lord, what shall I do?" The spiritual binds us in our humility, in our responsibility to heal and transform. A silence falls after we sing it a final time– together. I treasure that moment. My mind returns to it again and again.

Yet, something strange happens when the following week I stand in a circle of four women. As I start to say "my community loves and supports me," I actually bend over, holding back the sobs. I have to push myself to keep speaking, letting them know simultaneously my deepest longing and my deepest fear: My community loves and supports me; I am all alone and nobody cares.

I'm having lots of feelings in this Deeper Change forum on somatic conditioning. My circle of women who don't "know" me, wait for me to rise, to catch my breath. Together we stand shoulder to shoulder, outstretched arm to outstretched arm, embodying my newfound mantra. We are reconditioning my body to stand with both feet planted, rooted to this mantra—my community loves and supports me.

I say this to the young Amanda who believes the opposite; who chants the old mantra "I'm all alone and nobody cares." I say it to the lonely foster child who doesn't know why her mother left. I say it to the teen who's been rejected by two prospective adoptive families. I say it to the Black girl whose community has repeatedly told her she's too dark, too "African" to be beautiful.

What is your truth? Can you identify a simple phrase or sentence that strengthens and connects you? Maybe it's the opposite of that corrosive mantra that's accompanied you much of your life. If you are like me, then you will need to share that mantra in community for it to become real.

My community loves and supports me

I belong to community.

The community loves me. The

community supports me.

Acknowledgements

My community loves and supports me.

To those who have crossed over and passed on, I say thank you. This includes my mother Geraldine Kemp and my grandmother Olivia Kemp who are still pulling for me.

This book would not have been possible without the help of many, many people. Sudiksha Joshi first selected the essays and affirmed that they cohered. My business mastermind group, business buddy Debra Witt, and Ryan Elliason's course provided an empowering context for me to create and execute a plan for my business. Moreover, the first person to pre-order the book was in Ryan's course. My 1000+ friends on Facebook gave me great advice about the title and cover. This book would certainly not have been published without Matthew Armstead who coached me through numerous moments of overwhelm and provided a systems approach. Similarly Sonia Ahuja gave me the gift of her wonderful deep listening and incisive questions as I defined the community into which I write.

In the work of racial justice and oneness, two women loom large: Mary Wood, a white feminist and racial justice activist, taught at my high school and loved me and mentored me as I combined activism and school work. Niyonu Spann came late in my life, but her groundbreaking Beyond Diversity 101 intensives transformed how I saw myself and gave direction to my art. Her work as a composer, choral director, and organizational development guru continue to inspire me.

I am also grateful to my artistic and academic residency partners at Haverford College, Cambridge Friends School, Lancaster Theological Seminary, and Franklin & Marshall College. These schools have given me the space to create art, to reflect on my work and nurture young people. I will never forget Haverford College's female a capella group, The Outskirts, who accompanied me beautifully and with hardly any preparation.

Finally, because I grew up in foster care, family life is a real learning ground for me. I am deeply grateful to my husband Michael for allowing me to include examples from our lives together. My son Gabriel Anthony-Kemp, as usual, challenged and inspired me as a mother and an activist. Collectively our children motivated me to love more, laugh out loud and cry whenever I felt like it.

Thank you to all of you.

May our ancestors continue to watch over and give us that extra push whenever we need it.

About the Author

Dr. Amanda Kemp graduated from Stanford and Northwestern Universities where she majored in History and African & Afro-American Studies and earned a PhD in Performance Studies respectively.

She conducts racial justice, arts and academic residencies at schools and colleges throughout the U.S. She has performed, facilitated workshops, and guest lectured at educational institutions and faith gatherings for over 25,000 people over the last decade.

A gifted speaker, Dr. Kemp also shares her distinct brand of performance-lecture in which she incorporates poetry, film and music to teach African American history and culture. She has been the keynote speaker at many Dr. Martin Luther King Jr., Black History Month, and Women's History Month events at schools, and colleges.

Dr. Kemp also works as a diversity and justice consultant for organizations, evaluating programs and their policies, helping with strategic planning, and training staff to embody principles of diversity and inclusion. She leads workshops for non-profits such as: Self-care for People who Want to Change the World; Say the Wrong Thing; and How NOT to Be Tokenized When You are a Minority on a Board of Directors.

Poet, Performer, and Racial Justice Advocate

A lifelong poet, performer, and racial justice advocate, Dr. Kemp was awarded Stanford's prestigious Gardner Fellowship for Public Service. Kemp worked for the Honorable Maxine Waters and the Rev. Jesse Jackson and helped to lead the anti-apartheid divestment movement. She also helped organize a 10,000 person March on Sacramento, CA for education rights.

Dr. Kemp left politics to pursue a Ph.D. in performance studies at Northwestern University. While there, her interest in South Africa continued to grow, and she traveled to South Africa with the Ford Foundation where she did a report on the contemporary women's movement. Through getting involved with jazz and music in South Africa, she rediscovered her creative voice that she felt she lost her first few years in graduate school. In South Africa she witnessed the historic elections of 1994, debuted her play "Sister Outsider" and co-founded a trio of women performance poets called "Intimate Dread." Reinvigorated from experiences in there, Dr. Kemp finished her dissertation which focused on African American and South African ties in the 1920s and 1930s, and has since taught at Cornell University, Dickinson College, and Franklin & Marshall College where she served as the chair of Africana Studies.

In 2008 Dr. Kemp founded Theater for Transformation to create performances that incorporated spirituality and ritual, history and song in an effort to transform people and communities. She is now touring INSPIRA: The Power of the Spiritual and has released two CDs related to that show. Her play "Show Me the Franklins: Benjamin Franklin, Slavery and the Ancestors" is available on DVD and is often used in classes. Other plays include "Sister Friend," for which there is also a CD, and "To Cross an Ocean Four Centuries Long" which can also be purchased or streamed.

She lives in Pennsylvania with her husband violinist Michael Jamanis, five children, a guinea pig, and a chocolate lab named Jake.

Work with Dr. Amanda Kemp

Residencies

Dr. Kemp offers two-day, three-day and five-day residencies that combine live performance, public lectures, classroom visits and a community performing arts showcase.

Send a query to amanda@dramandakemp.com.

Performances

Dr. Kemp is now touring INSPIRA: The Power of the Spiritual See www.dramandakemp.com for upcoming performances near you or send an email to info@theatrefortransformation.org

Workshops/Master Mind Groups

"Say the Wrong Thing" Workshops can be hosted by organizations and faith communities.

Send a query to amanda@dramandakemp.com.

Master Mind Book Discussion and Action Groups

Accepting applications to join online groups. Email
amanda@dramandakemp.com

Stay Connected

www.Twitter.com/dramandakemp
www.Facebook.com/dramandakemp

Also by Dr. Amanda Kemp

Videos

Show Me the Franklins! The Ancestors, Benjamin Franklin and Slavery

To Cross an Ocean Four Centuries Long: Slavery and the Nature of Hope

Sound Recordings

INSPIRA: The Power of the Spiritual Chaconne Emancipated

Phillis Wheatley From Africa to America and Beyond

Books

Show Me the Franklins! Remembering the Ancestors, Benjamin Franklin and Slavery (a play with footnotes)

Websites and Blog

www.dramandakemp.com
www.dramandkemp.bandcamp.com
www.dramandakemp.com/blog

Made in the USA
Monee, IL
29 September 2020